FIGHTING FOR THEIR COUNTRY:
MINORITIES AT WAR

Minority Soldiers Fighting in the Vietnam War

ELIZABETH SCHMERMUND

Cavendish Square
New York

Published in 2018 by Cavendish Square Publishing, LLC
243 5th Avenue, Suite 136, New York, NY 10016

First Edition

Website: cavendishsq.com

CPSIA Compliance Information: Batch #CS17CSQ

All websites were available and accurate when this book was sent to press.

Library of Congress Cataloging-in-Publication Data

Names: Schmermund, Elizabeth.
Title: Minority soldiers fighting in the Vietnam War / Elizabeth Schmermund.
Description: New York : Cavendish Square, 2018. | Series: Fighting for their country: minorities at war | Includes index.
Identifiers: ISBN 9781502626660 (library bound) | ISBN 9781502626608 (ebook)
Subjects: LCSH: Vietnam War, 1961-1975--African Americans--Juvenile literature.
Classification: LCC DS559.8.B55 S34 2018 | DDC 959.704'34--dc23

Editorial Director: David McNamara
Editor: Caitlyn Miller
Copy Editor: Alex Tessman
Associate Art Director: Amy Greenan
Designer: Stephanie Flecha
Production Coordinator: Karol Szymczuk
Photo Research: J8 Media

The photographs in this book are used by permission and through the courtesy of: Cover Co Rentmeester/The LIFE Picture Collection/Getty Images; p. 4 Zuma Press/Alamy Stock Photo; p. 10 Digital Image Library/Alamy Stock Photo; p. 15, 35, 81, 94 Bettmann/Getty Images; p. 17 Ed Clark/The LIFE Picture Collection; p. 20 William Lovelace/Hulton Archive/Getty Images; p. 23 Ed Kolenovsky/AP Images; p. 25 NARA/Wikimedia Commons/File:"Cmdr. Thomas A. Gaylord, USN (Ret'd), administers oath to five new Navy nurses commissioned in New York...", 03-08-1945 - NARA - 520618.jpg/Public Domain; p. 28 Pavalena/Shutterstock.com; p. 30 Corbis/Getty Images; p. 33 Keystone-France/Gamma-Rapho/Getty Images; p. 38 Holloway/AP Images; p. 43 Ronald L. Haeberle/The LIFE Images Collection/Getty Images; p. 47 Manuel Litran/Paris Match/Getty Images; p. 51, 55 Archive Photos/Getty Images; p. 52 Ted Spiegel/Corbis/Getty Images; p. 60 Natale Matteo/Shutterstock.com; p. 61 TAG Holdings LLC; p. 64 NARA; p. 66 U.S. Air Force Photo; p. 68 U.S. Military/File:HanoiHilton1973.JPEG/Public Domain; p. 72 Underwood Archives/Getty Images; p. 76 Rudi Williams/Department of Defense; p. 78 By Bill Wunsch/The Denver Post/Getty Images; p. 84 PhotoQuest/Getty Images; p. 86 Eddie Adams/AP Images; p. 91 Sean Pavone Photo/iStockphoto.com; p. 96 Brian Wickham/Wikimedia Commons/File:BG Charles J. Girard arrives in Saigon, March, 1969.jpg/Used with Permission.
Printed in the United States of America

CONTENTS

CAMP McCOY
American Servicemen's
war is not healthy for children and other living
COME HOME

A Controversial War

Today, the Vietnam War is often regarded as a dark period in American history. The United States entered the war when Vietnam was divided into two separate countries: North Vietnam and South Vietnam. North Vietnam was controlled by a **communist** government and was supported by communist nations, including the **Soviet Union**, while South Vietnam was anti-communist and was supported by democratic countries, including the United States. Beginning in November 1955, the war lasted nearly twenty years before ending on April 30, 1975. When entering the war, United States government officials never imagined that it would last so long. They also had no idea that it would cause such great destruction, both on the warfront and on the home front, with American confidence in the US government diminishing. During this drawn out and eventually unsuccessful war, 58,193 Americans were killed and over 150,000 were wounded. In addition, the

***Opposite*: Protesters gather to make their voices heard against the Vietnam War.**

war was very unpopular because of the style of fighting—called **guerilla warfare**—that was used in the war. Troops were ambushed with booby traps and fighters in disguise. Adding to the war's unpopularity, the United States began a **draft** to send young men into combat.

A draft is when a government forces certain citizens—usually through a lottery, or a random selection—to fight in a war. The Vietnam War draft began in 1969 and lasted until 1973. Many people did not believe in the war's cause and, thus, did not want to fight. But if they were chosen for the draft, they had to go. Approximately 2,215,000 men were drafted into military service during the period between 1964 and 1973. Many thousands also attempted to evade the draft and went into hiding. About 30,000 men went to Canada during this period so that they would not be drafted.

The draft disproportionately affected poor, working-class, and minority young men. Approximately 55 percent of American forces in Vietnam came from a working-class background, while 25 percent came from poorer socio-economic backgrounds. The war also disproportionately affected minority soldiers. While, at the time, African American men made up approximately 11 percent of the American population, nearly 13 percent of soldiers in the Vietnam War were African American. When it comes to fatalities, nearly 20 percent of all casualties during the height of the Vietnam War from 1965 to 1969 were black soldiers (25 percent in 1965). Due to this inequality, then-president Johnson ordered that the participation of African American soldiers should be cut in combat units. This effectively cut the casualty rate of black soldiers from 20 percent to less than 12 percent by 1969.

While the US government did not keep statistics of the number of Hispanic soldiers fighting in the war, subsequent analysis shows that they made up approximately 5.5 percent of all casualties during the war. This points to the fact that Hispanics were also overrepresented in casualties than in the general population, where they made up less than 5 percent of the population.

Due both to these inequities and to the general belief among Americans that Vietnam was a lost cause and one that American soldiers should not die for, many Americans protested the draft. Beginning in 1964, students would burn their draft cards in resistance of the war. They wrote to representatives and organized mass protests. In the last years of the war, there were many draft resisters. These people refused to serve on moral grounds. In 1972, there were more conscientious objectors than people called to serve. Overall, over 200,000 people were categorized as "delinquent," or they had not served although they had been drafted, throughout the war. Due to the conflicting beliefs of the American public, returning soldiers were often treated with disdain upon arriving back in the United States. They would be spit on or taunted and often did not receive public recognition for their service.

In addition to general public perception, African American soldiers experienced prejudice in the military—and also could feel more resentful at being compelled to serve for a country in which they were not even granted full rights due to their race. In 1966, President Johnson began a program called Project 100,000, which lowered the qualification standards for men to be drafted into the war. Previously, many African Americans who had perhaps not had a full education had been able to avoid the draft. However, with this program, they were no longer able to do so. Between 1966 and 1969, 41 percent of those drafted through this program were African Americans. Poor men and Hispanic men were also more likely to be drafted under this program.

Despite the public reception at home, many minority soldiers were highly decorated and well trained. Approximately twenty African American soldiers received the Medal of Honor for their service in Vietnam, which is the highest military honor given. Several African Americans were promoted to general, the highest rank in the army. Following the Vietnam War, African Americans made up an even higher percentage of the American military than previously. By 1976, they made up more than 15 percent of all those in the American military. However, proportionally, they remained underrepresented in the higher ranks; African American officers continued to account for less than 4 percent of all military officers.

Following the assassination of Martin Luther King Jr. on April 4, 1968, black Americans called even more strongly for their rights across one hundred cities in the United States. However, in Vietnam, many white soldiers celebrated his death and, in one case, even paraded around their military base in Ku Klux Klan robes. This led to racial conflict in Vietnam, which did not ease when the soldiers returned home.

The Vietnam War and the place of minorities in it, as well as the fight for civil rights back at home and the issues returning veterans faced, will be explored in this book. In chapters 2 and 3, Joseph B. Anderson and Norman Alexander McDaniel are profiled in order to examine their particular experiences during the war. It is important to note that different people had varying experiences during the war and one minority soldier's experience should not stand in for the experience of all minority service members. However, these experiences do give us a more in-depth view of the challenges and rewards that many minority service members experienced before, during, and after the Vietnam War.

WHITE
WAITING ROOM
ostal Telegraph
THE INTERNATIONAL SYSTEM
HERE
3
4
5
2
CHATT

ONE

Life at Home

The 1950s and 1960s were important decades in the United States and a period during which time civil rights were expanded to many different minority groups. In particular, black Americans achieved rights that they had never been granted before as American citizens. Other minority groups—including Latinos and women—also gained more legal rights than ever before. This did not happen easily or quickly. In fact, the entire **civil rights movement** took many years and involved protesting in the face of violence for these rights to be achieved. Men and women—including great civil rights leaders like Martin Luther King Jr.—lost their lives in this fight for equal rights. While the battle in Vietnam was raging, this equally important battle was being fought at home.

***Opposite*: In the Southern United States, racial segregation was an unfortunate reality until the passage of the 1964 Civil Rights Act.**

THE CIVIL RIGHTS MOVEMENT

The civil rights movement grew out of a response to unfair American laws against black Americans following the abolition of slavery in 1865, at the end of the Civil War. Although slavery was abolished after the Northern states won the Civil War in 1865, unequal and discriminatory practices continued. This was called the period of Jim Crow, which references the **Jim Crow laws** passed and enforced in the Southern United States that segregated white Americans from black Americans. This meant that blacks and whites had to attend different schools and eat in different restaurants, or parts of restaurants. During this time, it was not unusual to see signs posted everywhere around a town that said, "Whites Only—No Blacks."

Plessy v. Ferguson

Although this sounds unquestionably discriminatory today, segregation was actually deemed legal in the US court system and was a largely accepted—at least, for whites—part of American, and particularly, Southern society. In 1896, a Supreme Court case called *Plessy v. Ferguson* cemented segregation. In this case, a mixed-race man named Homer Plessy sat in a "whites only" car while riding a train from New Orleans to Convington, Louisiana. Plessy was one-eighth African but was considered black under Louisiana state laws and, thus, was required to sit in the so-called "colored" car. Plessy chose his seat knowingly as an act of resistance against segregation. He knew he would likely be arrested—and he was.

In the court case that followed, Plessy's lawyers argued that that his rights, as dictated by the Thirteenth and Fourteenth

Amendments to the American Constitution, had been violated. The Thirteenth Amendment had abolished slavery in 1865, while the Fourteenth Amendment gave all citizens, no matter their race, equal protection under the law. Plessy's lawyers argued that segregation in Louisiana meant that he, as a black man, was treated differently than a white man—and, thus, that he was not granted equal protection. Eventually, *Plessy v. Ferguson* went to the Supreme Court of the United States (Ferguson was the name of the first judge who heard the case in Louisiana and who initially ruled against Plessy). The US Supreme Court is the highest court in the United States and gives final determination on cases that are heard by lower courts throughout the nation.

The Supreme Court heard the case and eventually handed down a decision that Plessy was indeed guilty. However, this case wasn't just about Plessy. The case was about whether or not Jim Crow laws and racial segregation in the United States would be held up by federal law as constitutional. In their famous determination, the Supreme Court judges decided seven to one that racial segregation did not deprive black Americans of their rights under the Constitution due to what became known as the **"separate but equal" doctrine**. According to this doctrine, separate facilities for black and white Americans were constitutional (and, thus, segregation was constitutional) as long as what was provided was approximately equal for both races. This ruling would set the stage for additional segregation laws that were passed in following years and Jim Crow became more entrenched in the American South.

Following this ruling, many more public facilities became segregated. Voter registration was also made more difficult for both African Americans and poor whites through laws that made voters pay fines or take literacy tests. This effectively **disenfranchised** African Americans—as well as poor whites—from the political process. Unable to vote for their representatives, they remained unrepresented in the American political system. This instituted systemic racism with the explicit intent to create a white, middle-class electorate that would vote based on their needs while blocking or ignoring the needs of African Americans and other minority groups.

Lynchings and Violence against African Americans

Segregation and voter suppression would remain common practice for many years. Lynchings also occurred during this time, during which black men in particular were killed and their murderers were not held accountable. In one famous and tragic case, a fourteen-year-old boy named Emmett Till was accused of "flirting" with a white woman in a grocery store in Money, Mississippi, in 1955. Reports differ as to whether or not Till said anything to Carolyn Bryant, a white woman in the store, although an impartial witness later said that Till had done nothing "inappropriate." Whatever the case, a week later, when Bryant's husband returned home from a work trip, his wife told him that Till had flirted with her. Bryant went in search of Till with his half-brother, eventually kidnapping Till from his bed in the early morning. For hours, Bryant and others beat Till until he was nearly dead; then, they shot him by the bank of the Tallahatchie River, weighted his body, and threw him into the water. Emmett Till's mother insisted on an open-casket funeral for her young son to show the physical damage that had been done to him.

While Bryant and his half-brother did go to court for their role in the murder of Till, an all-white jury soon acquitted them after deliberating for a little over an hour and they were released. One of the jurors supposedly said, "If we hadn't stopped to drink pop, it wouldn't have taken so long."

While Emmett Till's tragic case became very famous, it was far from isolated in the South. Black men and boys in particular were often killed with impunity by whites. Even if

The brutal lynching of fourteen-year-old Emmett Till drew attention to the violence and discrimination African Americans faced.

their murderers were brought to trial, they were almost always acquitted by all-white juries.

Brown v. Board of Education of Topeka, Kansas

In response to not only the social inequity but the violence that many black Americans faced, the civil rights movement began to gain momentum. Groups such as the National Association for the Advancement of Colored People (NAACP) fought against discriminatory policies against African Americans through litigation and lobbying. One of the greatest victories that began a new era of civil rights was the Supreme Court case *Brown v. Board of Education of Topeka, Kansas*, in 1954. *Brown v. Board of Education*, as it became known, began as a class action lawsuit against the Board of Education of Topeka, Kansas, by thirteen parents on behalf of their children. They stated that their young children were not receiving a fair education due to the school district's policy of racial segregation. Oliver Brown, who was named in the lawsuit, argued that his daughter, Linda, had to travel much farther away to a "black only" school when a "white" school was just down the block from their home. The facilities for white students and the materials they were given, particularly books, were much better than those reserved for black students.

The NAACP's chief counsel, Thurgood Marshall, argued the case in front of the Supreme Court. Eventually, the Supreme Court unanimously agreed that segregation in public schools was unconstitutional, effectively overturning the policy of "separate but equal" that had been established in *Plessy v. Ferguson*. The decision read, in part:

Thurgood Marshall (*center*) speaks after winning the landmark case *Brown v. Board of Education of Topeka, Kansas.*

Segregation of white and colored children in public schools has a detrimental effect upon the colored children. The effect is greater when it has the sanction of the law, for the policy separating the races is usually interpreted as denoting the inferiority of the negro group. A sense of inferiority affects the motivation of a child to learn … We conclude that, in the field of public education, the doctrine of "separate but equal" has no place. Separate educational facilities are inherently unequal. Therefore, we hold that the plaintiffs

Dr. Martin Luther King Jr. leads marchers from Selma to Montgomery in March 1965.

continued to ignore national legislation, such as the Civil Rights Act, and continued racially discriminatory practices. During these three organized marches in February and March 1965, protesters were beaten and even killed by local police. Finally, President Lyndon Johnson sent in thousands of US soldiers to protect the activists during their march. On March 24, 25,000 people entered into the capital city of Montgomery in support of voting rights.

CIVIL RIGHTS AND VIETNAM

The civil rights movement coincided with an escalation of American troops in Vietnam. This meant that the problems many African Americans faced at home in the United States were transferred to the war in Vietnam, as was their resistance against unfair treatment. This was especially true because the Vietnam War was the first time in American history that African Americans fought side by side in racially integrated units with whites for the duration of a war. While black Americans had long fought for their country alongside white soldiers, before they had always been deployed in racially segregated units—black soldiers with black soldiers and white soldiers with white soldiers. Although some segregated units still existed in Vietnam, they were much more rare than before. This was an important move toward equality, yet it also could cause tensions between white and black soldiers in Vietnam.

The difficulties these African American soldiers faced were not new. After World War II, two million black soldiers arrived home from fighting against Nazism in Europe and the South Pacific. They expected to return home to greater rights given to them, particularly in light of their sacrifice for their country. However, this was not the case. Their fight for equal rights provided an important catalyst for the civil rights movement. These groups included the Congress of Racial Equality, also known as CORE, which would go on to lead protests, boycotts, and sit-ins. Soldiers returning home from Vietnam would experience similar problems and would similarly fight for their rights.

In spite of these obstacles, many African Americans felt it was their duty to serve in Vietnam. Remembering the words of African American activist and historian W. E. B. Du Bois during World War I, many African Americans gladly fought in the Vietnam War: "Let us, while the war lasts, forget our special grievances and close ranks shoulder to shoulder with our white fellow citizens … fighting for democracy. We make no ordinary sacrifice, but we make it gladly and willingly." They wanted to fight for their country and "prove" their value for their country—even if it meant sacrificing their lives.

But the Vietnam era was a very different time in American history. The draft disproportionately affected African American and poor whites in the southern United States, who were statistically more likely to support segregation than white Americans in other parts of the country. Draft boards would pick the numbers randomly assigned to men who would be conscripted into the military to go to Vietnam. Yet in most areas, no African Americans were present on draft boards, meaning they were without any representation whatsoever. Some African Americans who grew up in segregation or in conditions of poverty thought that the war would be an escape for them and so they signed up voluntarily. This meant that many more African Americans were sent to war than white Americans, based on the general population of the United States. And this fueled a new and unsettling rumor in the 1960s: the Vietnam War was a genocide against black Americans orchestrated by the American government.

Of course, while great discrimination did exist against African Americans both during the draft and across the United States at this time, there was no orchestrated plot. But the

Boxing legend Muhammad Ali spent time in prison after he refused to be drafted to Vietnam.

effect was the same. Many of those involved in the civil rights movement urged black Americans not to go to war. Martin Luther King Jr. encouraged African Americans to become conscientious objectors and refuse to fight for the "greatest purveyor of violence" in the world. Famous black icons like Muhammad Ali did so and were gravely punished for their actions. When Ali refused the draft, he was sent to prison and stripped of his world boxing title.

Phyllis Mae Dailey

During World War II, many African Americans enlisted or were drafted into the military despite the fact that they were subjected to segregation not only during their service but upon returning at military parades and even in military transportation. In January 1941, the first African American women were allowed to join the army as nurses due to the increased need for those with medical training on the warfront. African American women, like African American men serving, often were given not only separate but unequal rations and living quarters on the bases. They would have substandard equipment and eat inferior food. They were also subjected to racism both from some of the white women they served with and from injured soldiers they were aiding.

In 1945, the navy allowed African American women to join its ranks for the first time. The first African American woman sworn into the navy was named Phyllis Mae Dailey. A graduate of Columbia University in New York, Dailey stated that she "knew barriers were going to be broken down eventually and felt the more applicants, the better the chances would be for each person." Unfortunately, only three other African American women would follow Dailey's footsteps by being sworn into the navy as nurses. Dailey stayed in the service even following the war, becoming the first African American woman to join the regular service in 1948 and then the first African American

Phyllis Mae Dailey (*second from right*) receives her commission in 1945.

navy nurse to serve outside the continental United States in Hawaii. While the navy stopped excluding recruits based on race in 1945, they still had a long way to go. At the end of the war, only four women, including Dailey, were part of the Navy Nurse Corps compared with six thousand African American women in the Women's Army Corps.

CHINA
HANOI
Haiphong
Nam Định
LAOS
Gulf of
Tonkin
Vinh
Hainan Isla
Huế
THAILAND
Da Nang
VIETNAM
Qui Nhon
CAMBODIA
Nha Trang
Ho Chi Minh City
Gulf of
Thailand
Cần Thơ
Vũng Tàu
South
China Sea

TWO

The Vietnam War

The country of Vietnam has a long and complex history, which explains why the country experienced such a long and bloody civil war. Located on the eastern Indochina Peninsula in Southeast Asia, Vietnam had been colonized by France from 1862 until the end of World War II in 1945. Originally separated into different colonies, the nation was officially declared French Indochina in 1887. The main reason the French wanted to colonize the country was because it was rich in many natural resources. French settlers developed a plantation economy and grew and exported tobacco, indigo, tea, and coffee, among other crops that could be easily grown in the country's tropical climate. But, as in many other colonized countries, the French also instituted many cultural changes for the Vietnamese. They converted many people to Roman Catholicism and forced them to learn French in a Western-style educational system. In addition, a hierarchy developed in which

***Opposite*:** **The Socialist Republic of Vietnam, as it is known today, is the easternmost section of the Indochina Peninsula in Southeast Asia and borders the South China Sea.**

the native Vietnamese were treated as less than the French colonists there. Colonists received special treatment from the French government and often hired Vietnamese to work on their plantations for poor pay and unfair—and sometimes even brutal—treatment.

THE FIRST INDOCHINA WAR

Eventually Vietnamese nationalist movements began, led by such figures as Ho Chi Minh, who wanted to expel the French from their country and institute self-rule. Although there were skirmishes here and there, the French continued to

Ho Chi Minh, seated here at a youth rally, would become a nationalist leader and the Communist president of North Vietnam.

have control over the country until World War II broke out in 1940. That year, the Japanese invaded French Indochina, which they controlled until 1945. During this time, Ho Chi Minh created the **Viet Minh**, roughly translated as the League for the Independence of Vietnam, to fight against both Japanese and French colonial forces.

This was a time of great difficulty for the Vietnamese, who were living under two colonial powers. During this period, a great famine spread across the country as well, killing up to two million people from starvation. The French administration in Vietnam badly mismanaged the country during this time, largely provoking the famine, and did not properly respond to the crisis. When the Japanese left the country in 1945, the French-educated Emperor Bao Dai was left in control of the country. However, because Bao Dai was viewed as a puppet to the French, Ho Chi Minh and the Viet Minh began organized attacks to take control of the country.

In March of that year, the Viet Minh told their fellow Vietnamese to steal food from rice warehouses and to refuse to pay their taxes in an effort to survive—as well as to fight against the government. Then, the Viet Minh attacked and seized the city of Hanoi in the north of the country. They declared the Democratic Republic of Vietnam (DRV) as separate from the southern part of the country, ruled over by Emperor Bao Dai from Saigon. Ho Chi Minh was named the new president of the republic. Fearful that they would lose control of the country, the French set up the state of South Vietnam in 1949 and backed Bao's rule there. This began the First Indochina War, which would last ten years and pit the Viet Minh against the French from 1946 until 1956. Soon after Ho Chi Minh declared the republic from Hanoi, the Viet Minh were forced from the city. Gradually, throughout the end of the 1940s and the early 1950s, the Viet Minh captured large swaths of land across rural Vietnam.

The Viet Minh were largely backed by the population and rose to power on a wave of nationalism against colonial exploitation of Vietnam. They also received initial support and funding from the United States, the Soviet Union, and the Republic of China due to their opposition to the Japanese during the war. There were many communists in the Viet Minh. The Communist Party had been repressed in Vietnam under French rule, and they had fervently spoken out against the colonial powers. They became important new players during the First Indochina War. Eventually, the Viet Minh were succeeded by the Lien Viet, or the Vietnamese National Popular Front.

By the 1950s, the French were losing the war in Vietnam. Leaders of other countries had hesitated on whether or not to militarily engage on the side of the French. President Dwight D. Eisenhower publically stated that the United States would only militarily aid the French if the British would do so as well. However, the British did not want to get involved. In 1953, the Viet Minh even began to take over the neighboring country of Laos, a French ally. Then, in late 1953, the French forces occupied the Dien Bien Phu valley, which was then rapidly made into an important military base with an airstrip. The Viet Minh gathered their troops and hid artillery in the caves around the valley. In early 1954, they began engaging the French militarily. It was a decisive victory for the Viet Minh, who overran the French base in May of that year. The French were shocked and devastated.

The tide of public opinion began to change in France and French prime minister Pierre Mendes was able to pass a resolution through the parliament that officially withdrew the French from the country. As part of the Geneva Conference in 1954, a ceasefire was negotiated and independence was given to Cambodia, Laos, and Vietnam from French control. Vietnam was also partitioned into two separate zones: the northern zone would be governed by the Viet Minh and the southern zone would be governed by the State of Vietnam and Emperor

The Viet Minh arrive in Hanoi in 1945, where they would declare the Democratic Republic of Vietnam as separate from the southern part of the country.

Bao Dai. They planned that another conference, held in two years' time, that would work to establish a unified Vietnam through general elections. For a three hundred–day period, Vietnamese citizens would be able to freely travel between the two countries at the 17th parallel line of latitude (the border that separated the two countries) before the border would be closed. Many northern Vietnamese fled to South Vietnam during this time, fearful of being governed by the communist Viet Minh. Conversely, approximately 52,000 Vietnamese traveled from the south to the north during this time.

A DIVIDED COUNTRY

As the Viet Minh ruled freely over North Vietnam, tales of their excesses began to spread. There was significant political oppression during this time and executions were carried out against critics of the government. The American government actively worked to spread **propaganda** against the communist government during this time. In fact, the allied powers deliberately held off on immediate elections because they were fearful that the Vietnamese would vote to unify the country under a communist regime.

This was during a period of time called the **Cold War**, during which the Soviet Union and the United States positioned themselves ideologically and politically against one another. The Soviet Union was ruled under a communist government while the United States was the beacon of democracy. The United States grew fearful of growing communism throughout the global community and fought against the Soviet Union to restrict their territories. President Eisenhower coined the term "the domino theory" during this time. He meant that if one

President Ngo Dinh Diem took control of South Vietnam in 1955.

country in a region fell to communism the other countries in the region were in danger of falling to communism, too. This would shift the balance of power in the favor of the Soviet Union and against the United States, and it was something the United States government worked actively against.

In the State of Vietnam, political oppression was growing as well. Ngo Dinh Diem, named prime minister by Bao Dai in 1954, ousted Dai from power and took control of the country. He then launched a campaign in 1955 to hunt down, capture, torture, and execute any Vietnamese who were linked to communist activities. Between 1955 and 1957, around twelve thousand suspected communists were killed; by the end of 1958, approximately forty thousand had been jailed. Diem became an ally to the United States and was invited to the country on an official tour in 1957. However, the situation in Vietnam was rapidly deteriorating.

From 1957 until 1959, uprisings occurred throughout South Vietnam. At first, the South Vietnamese government did not view these uprisings as a threat to their government. However, by 1959, they did and passed a severely restrictive law that made anything deemed political violence punishable by death. Diem called those involved in the uprisings the **Viet Cong**, alluding to the belief that they were "communist traitors" to their country. In late 1960, those who opposed Diem in South Vietnam formed an organization called the National Liberation Front. Many of its members were not communists and were just opposed to the political oppression that had become standard under Diem. However, American officials grew frightened that they were under the control of the North Vietnamese communists. In response to this fear, the US government increased military aid to South Vietnam and Diem, although they did not yet agree upon a large-scale military intervention. However, by 1962, nine thousand American troops were stationed in South Vietnam. This was done mainly under the presidency of John F. Kennedy, who was fearful of the political risks of losing the entire country to a communist government and an ally to the Soviet Union. As he escalated troops in the region, his advisor told him that they were in "danger [that] we shall replace the French as a colonial force in the area and bleed as the French did."

The Viet Cong were against the presence of the American military in their country. They also gained larger support from Vietnamese peasants, who suffered economically under Diem's policies, and those who suffered under the political oppression. Many Buddhists in Vietnam were similarly angry at Diem for policies that aided Catholics in the country while discriminating against other religions.

In 1963, Diem was killed in a coup by his own generals just several weeks before President Kennedy's assassination. The US government was, at first, happy that Diem had been ousted. But soon chaos engulfed the country. North Vietnam began to actively aid the South Vietnamese rebels during the political instability that ensued. In very quick succession, several different military governments grabbed power of South Vietnam before being toppled. President Lyndon B. Johnson, who had taken over the US presidency after Kennedy's assassination, grew convinced that US military intervention was needed to prevent the country from being taken over by the communist north.

AN ESCALATION TO WAR

Then, in August 1964, the US government claimed that two North Vietnamese torpedo boats attacked US destroyers in the Gulf of Tonkin. This attack was used as motivation for the US Congress to pass the **Gulf of Tonkin Resolution** on August 7. The resolution allowed President Johnson, without a formal declaration of war by Congress, to use military force in Vietnam. Later, declassified documents showed that the North Vietnamese had not attacked the US destroyers first—if at all. This was seen mostly as an excuse for getting into a war that was still controversial and contested by the American

The US aircraft carrier *Bon Homme Richard* sails in the Gulf of Tonkin in March 1968.

public. After the passage of the Gulf of Tonkin Resolution, in February 1965, the US military began bombing raids on North Vietnam. These bombings were referred to by the US military as "Operating Rolling Thunder."

In March, Johnson formally decided to enter into war with North Vietnam through sending in US combat forces. The American public mainly agreed with this decision. In June 1965, 82,000 US combat troops were stationed in Vietnam in order to aid the South Vietnamese against the North Vietnamese. By the end of July, Johnson had ordered an increase of 100,000 US combat troops. By the end of that year, another 100,000 combat troops were ordered to deploy to Vietnam. It would be the start of a very long and costly war.

US troops, under the command of General William Westmoreland, were engaged in a ground war in order to fight the North Vietnamese. The goal of troops on the ground was to kill as many enemy combatants as possible. Supported by air strikes above, they would go into regions called "free-fire zones" under the assumption that all civilians had already evacuated from the area. With the aid of air forces, they would coordinate heavy **shelling**, devastating the region and anyone inside it. Vietnamese civilians attempted to flee into refugee camps near Saigon and other "safer" cities. However, there were many civilian casualties. One of the reasons for this new tactic, which ultimately failed, was that the Viet Cong had instituted a policy of guerilla warfare and relied more and more on hit and run attacks and ambushes. This turned the tide of the war, causing psychological damage to American troops who felt constantly under attack and were not used to this style of warfare. It also resulted in increased US casualties.

Vietnam is known as one of the first "televised wars," meaning that American journalists filmed the war front and broadcast these images to the screens of Americans back home. In 1965, CBS News correspondent Morley Safer filmed a report showing US Marines using their cigarettes to burn down civilian huts in the Vietnamese village of Cam Ne. This was one of the few reports of the time that showed the negative side of US military force in Vietnam, but it was at the forefront of critical reporting.

Gradually, these reports—and continued escalation of troops—would turn the American public against the war. American soldiers returned home physically and psychologically damaged. American activists also worried about the fates of Vietnamese civilians. By November 1967, 500,000 American troops were stationed in Vietnam, 15,058 US military members had been killed, and 109,527 Americans had been wounded in Vietnam. Around that time, tens of thousands of protesters gathered outside the Pentagon in Washington, DC, to protest against continued American involvement in Vietnam. It was one of the first outward signs of the public outcry that would come to define the rest of the war.

THE TET OFFENSIVE

Then, in January 1969, the **Tet Offensive** began. Named after the lunar new year, North Vietnamese forces, under the command of General Vo Nguyen Giap, coordinated attacks all across South Vietnam. This string of over one hundred attacks surprised the South Vietnamese and their US allies. Eventually they were able to take back most of the towns and cities that the North Vietnamese had taken over. However, during their occupation, the North Vietnamese forces executed thousands of people, most notably in the city of Hue. There nearly five thousand men, women, and children were killed. This further shocked the American public, who previously believed that they and their South Vietnamese allies were in control of the war and were easily winning against the North Vietnamese. The initial success of the Tet Offensive showed that, in fact, they were fighting against a formidable—and ruthless—opponent.

Due in part to the renewed public outcry, President Johnson decided to stop bombings across North Vietnam following the Tet Offensive, although bombings continued in the south and the ground war continued. He also publically promised that he would seek a path toward peace. Peace talks between the US and North Vietnam began in May of that year. They did not get very far.

POLITICS AND WAR

Johnson was running for reelection in 1968. However, in March of that year, he shocked the American people by withdrawing from the race, declaring,

> *With America's sons in the fields far away, with America's future under challenge right here at home, with our hopes and the world's hopes for peace in the balance every day, I do not believe that I should devote an hour or a day of my time to any personal partisan causes or to any duties other than the awesome duties of this office—the presidency of your country. Accordingly, I shall not seek, and I will not accept, the nomination of my party for another term as your President.*

Johnson was not only referring to the Vietnam War in his reasoning why he would not seek a second term; he was also referring to the tenuous racial relations in the country. On April 4, 1968, Martin Luther King Jr. was fatally shot after delivering a speech in Memphis. Rioting followed the great civil rights leader's assassination. All around the country, the demand for civil rights was growing louder.

The next November, Richard Nixon won the presidential election and prepared for his position at the White House. Upon taking office that January, Nixon planned on renewing support among the American public for the war, particularly by appealing to what he called "**the silent majority**." The silent majority were those who supposedly supported the Vietnam War, although they were not vocal in their beliefs. As Nixon's vice president would claim in 1969, "It is time for America's silent majority to stand up for its rights, and let us remember the American majority includes every minority. America's silent majority is bewildered by irrational protests."

Nixon planned on withdrawing troops gradually from Vietnam in order to prevent further American casualties, while increasing US air campaigns against North Vietnam. He also began a policy of what he called **Vietnamization**, which would focus on developing South Vietnamese military power so that they could fight their own ground war against the North Vietnamese with less support from US troops. Nixon also continued peace talks with the North Vietnamese in Paris, though they were at a standstill. The North Vietnamese would not declare peace until the US withdrew completely from Vietnam.

THE MY LAI MASSACRE

While the US government continued to work toward peace, the war seemed to be spiraling out of control in Vietnam. On November 12, 1969, journalist Seymour Hersh broke a heartbreaking story about a massacre that had taken place in the South Vietnamese village of My Lai the year before on March 16, 1968. My Lai was located about 100 miles (160.9 km)

The war crimes committed by US soldiers in My Lai would shock and outrage the world and lead to an even greater outcy against the Vietnam War.

southeast of a US army base and had a small population of around seven hundred inhabitants.

On the morning of March 16, three **platoons** of US troops landed in the village, where they had been ordered to conduct a "search and destroy" mission. This meant that they expected to find Viet Cong members in the village and were expected to do three things: search out the enemy in a certain location, destroy (kill) them, and then immediately leave the area. This had become an important and well-used tactic by the US military in the Vietnamese War, particularly when it was often so difficult to determine who were enemy combatants. The troops who landed at My Lai were told that there was a very active Viet Cong group in the region. These troops had also experienced grave suffering during the war and had sustained forty casualties since they had arrived in Vietnam three months earlier. They were told to destroy everything in the village—from livestock, to food, to wells, to homes, as well as any potential enemy combatants they came across.

Before the attacks, the troops were told that civilians would leave the village to go to a popular market and only Viet Cong members and sympathizers would remain. The captain of the troops was quoted by a soldier as saying: "Anybody that was running from us, hiding from us, or appears to be the enemy [was their enemy]. If a man was running, shoot him, sometimes even if a woman with a rifle was running, shoot her."

However, there were not enemy combatants in the village on that day. The only people in the village that morning were regular men, women, and children. Around one hundred soldiers from Charlie **Company** entered the village that morning. After their helicopters landed, they began firing at people working in the rice paddies and walking to and from the village. Then they gathered up large groups of villagers and led them into the center of the village. This is where the greatest massacre occurred. At some point, the soldiers began firing on the unarmed and unresisting civilians. They threw grenades at them and stabbed them with bayonets. Whole families were killed, including children, many of them infants and toddlers. As one soldier reported about the massacre,

> *I saw them shoot an M79 [grenade launcher] into a group of people who were still alive. But it was mostly done with a machine gun. They were shooting women and children just like anybody else. We met no resistance and I only saw three captured weapons. We had no casualties. It was just like any other Vietnamese village—*

old papa-sans, women and kids. As a matter of fact, I don't remember seeing one military-age male in the entire place, dead or alive.

A helicopter pilot, Hugh Thompson Jr., who was flying over My Lai when the massacre occurred stopped to see if he could help the injured civilians he saw. When he asked a US soldier holding a machine gun if he could help the injured Vietnamese he saw on the ground, the soldier responded that he would "put them out of their misery." Thompson understood that something was very wrong. He, along with the men under his command, immediately attempted to rescue any remaining civilians. Thompson and his men were responsible for ending the massacre.

At the end of what would become known as the My Lai massacre, hundreds of innocent men, women, and children—including whole families—had been killed. The local Vietnamese government estimated that 504 civilians had been killed that day, while the US Army still contends that 347 were killed. When Hersh broke his story, after extensive interviewing with soldiers who had been there and who had tried to stop the events from unfolding, the American public was shocked. A Congressional inquiry was held and those who were in command on that day were court-martialed, although only one high-ranking official was put on trial (and eventually acquitted). Only one soldier was ever convicted for his role in the massacre. But, as journalist Jonathan Schell wrote, in that region of South Vietnam, up to 70 percent of villages had been completely destroyed and over 50,000 civilians were killed each year in the war. He wrote, "There can be no doubt that such an atrocity was possible only because a number of other methods of killing and destroying their villages had come to be the rule, and not the exception, in our conduct of the war."

For his part, the one soldier who was convicted of war crimes, Lieutenant William Calley, stated, "When my troops were getting massacred and mauled by an enemy I couldn't see, an enemy I couldn't feel, I couldn't touch … nobody in the military system ever described [the South Vietnamese] as anything other than Communist."

This horrific massacre was a stark reminder of the cost of the Vietnam War—paid by both the Vietnamese (North and South) as well as Americans. The war had become such a bloody guerilla battle, in which troops were so traumatized, that massacres like this became more commonplace. The American people saw Vietnam vets returning home from the war both psychologically and physically broken. Many of them relied on drugs to treat the pain of what they had experienced, and many of them were never the same again. This became a wake-up call for those who continued to support the war: the price was too great for both sides to continue. It must stop.

GRADUAL WITHDRAWAL

Richard Nixon's process of Vietnamization began the slow withdrawal of US troops from Vietnam. With Nixon's reelection in 1972, this process began to pick up speed. In January 1973, Nixon announced that the US military would no longer conduct any offensive action against the North Vietnamese. Later that month on January 27, the US, North Vietnam, and South Vietnam, along with South Vietnamese rebel groups, signed the Paris Peace Accords. This officially brought US involvement in

On March 3, 1973, the Paris Peace Accords were signed, effectively bringing US involvement in the Vietnam War to an end.

Asian American Veterans of the Vietnam War

Asian Americans faced unique challenges when fighting in the Vietnam War for their country. During the war, 35,000 Asian Americans were deployed to South Vietnam. According to Lily Lee Adams, a Veterans Administration nurse who counseled many returning Asian American veterans, "We discovered Asian Americans had unique problems—discrimination, getting beat up, getting called names, getting shot at." In one case, David Oshiro, a Japanese American, was injured and bleeding on the battlefield. However, those who came to rescue him did not believe that he was an American and refused to treat him at first. Only when he showed them his dog tags were they willing to evacuate him. "They'll get all the black and white guys before they get the Asians out," he said.

Another soldier remembers being called racial slurs and being threatened with a bayonet against his throat by one of his fellow soldiers. Years later, he still remembers the trauma of the racism he experienced within his military unit. However, special relationships were forged even in the face of these racist assaults. "A lot of times, black soldiers took [Asian soldiers] in, protected them, made friends with them," Adams says, "versus people of other ethnic backgrounds who were not as understanding of what was going on."

the Vietnam War to an end. Negotiations had been conducted since 1968, and this treaty was the fruit of these long years of diplomatic talks. The treaty stated that a ceasefire would begin later that day and the US troops would begin to withdraw fully within the next sixty days. During this time, US prisoners of war would be released by the North Vietnamese. It also stated that negotiations would continue between North and South Vietnam, with the aim of an eventual reunification of the country "through peaceful means."

While the United States had successfully negotiated its withdrawal from the war, the fighting within Vietnam would continue. In 1975, North Vietnam conducted attacks on South Vietnam that ended South Vietnamese independence. On July 2, 1976, North and South Vietnam were reunited to form the Socialist Republic of Vietnam. For many American veterans, this was the final straw. The war they had fought so hard for had ended in failure. In fact, the years of fighting and the many casualties suffered on both sides hadn't changed the transfer of power in Vietnam to communist forces. In 1977, President Jimmy Carter pardoned all so-called draft dodgers, allowing them to return home to the United States without consequence. However, many Vietnam veterans would continue to suffer for years following the end of the war.

THREE

Lieutenant Colonel Joseph B. Anderson

During the Vietnam War, minority soldiers fought with valor and were integral to the war effort. Lieutenant Colonel Joseph B. Anderson Jr. is one such African American soldier, and his leadership would eventually earn him a Silver Star.

Joseph was born the youngest of four children to Pearl and Joseph B. Anderson Sr. in Topeka, Kansas. His father worked on the Santa Fe railroad, and his mother was a homemaker. During this time, much of Topeka was still segregated. Before the *Brown v. Board of Education of Topeka, Kansas*, decision, the schools that Joseph B. Anderson Jr. attended were segregated. However, as he reached middle and high school, following the

***Opposite*: Joseph B. Anderson and his platoon were featured in the Pierre Schoendoerffer documentary *The Anderson Platoon* in 1967.**

momentous Supreme Court decision, the schools Anderson attended were integrated and he attended with white students as well.

WEST POINT

Anderson did well in these integrated schools, eventually becoming class president during his freshman year of high school and excelling in a variety of academic subjects and sports. Anderson did so well, in fact, that he caught the attention of admissions officers at the famed West Point, otherwise known as the United States Military Academy (USMA). Located in West Point, New York, this academy is the foremost military

Members of the honor guard march at the US Military Academy at West Point, where Anderson attended college.

academy in the United States. In order to be admitted, potential students need to receive a nomination from a member of Congress or another important political figure. In return for free tuition and a degree, **cadets**, as West Point students are known, are required to serve active duty in the military following their graduation. Out of Anderson's accepted class of nine hundred students, only nine African American students entered West Point. At his time of graduation, he was one of four graduating African American cadets in a class of 596 students total.

Anderson said that despite these obstacles, he was not insecure or overly worried about his status as an African American among many white cadets. He said that he had been very comfortable in his integrated high school and assumed that West Point would be no different. However, what was especially challenging for Anderson at West Point was the extreme discipline that was required of all cadets. They had to complete many drills and teachers were especially difficult on younger cadets to test if they could deal with the stress of being in active service in the military.

Anderson quickly excelled at West Point, too. He was named a Battalion Commander during his first year. He also said that he was very happy with his fellow classmates and cadets and stated that he did not experience racial discrimination during his time there. However, when Anderson's class went to visit other military bases in the South, he would feel the weight of segregation and discrimination. Despite Anderson's belief that he was treated mostly equally to white soldiers, there was one moment when he felt he was discriminated against at West Point. During his final year at the academy, Anderson believed that he was passed up for taking on a leadership role in his class because he was African American. The institution just "wasn't ready" for African American leaders, Anderson said. While a cadet, Anderson spent two months in Uganda with Operation Crossroads Africa, a nonprofit organization that sends youth volunteers to Africa to aid in development programs. When he returned back to West Point, proud of his experiences volunteering in Uganda, a commanding officer explicitly told Anderson that he would not be able to have any leadership opportunities because he had participated in this program. While it remained largely unstated, Anderson knew that this had more to do with his race than his capabilities or the fact that he had decided to volunteer over that summer.

VIETNAM AND *THE ANDERSON PLATOON*

Anderson graduated from West Point in 1965 with a degree in math and engineering, and as a commissioned second lieutenant, just as ground troops were being sent to Vietnam. Indeed, Anderson was soon sent to Vietnam—after graduating with honors from Airborne and Ranger School at Fort Bragg—where he would spent two **tours** as a platoon leader. During his first tour, Anderson would gain fame while being profiled in a documentary called *The Anderson Platoon*, directed by Pierre Schoendoerffer. The film would go on to win an Oscar for best feature-length documentary and would become a classic of Vietnam War film. Schoendoerffer embedded with the platoon from August 1, 1965, until October of the next year and filmed their daily lives. He chose Anderson's platoon, in particular, because he was interested in profiling a thirty-three-member platoon led by a twenty-four-year-old black man. This was the first war in which white American troops could be commanded

Viewers were intrigued by *The Anderson Platoon*, which showed an integrated platoon commanded by a black platoon leader.

by a black officer. Schoendoerffer wanted to show this reality to the general public.

The film follows Anderson as he leads patrols in search-and-destroy missions across Vietnam as part of "Operation Irving." Schoendoerffer does not glorify the war—in fact, the director has been described as generally "anti-war"—but his film shows the humanity of the soldiers and allowed American audiences to see the role of African American platoon leaders during the war. As depicted in the film, in the summer of 1965, shortly after Anderson arrived in Vietnam, Anderson and his platoon left a relatively safe base on a hilltop to conduct their mission. The film shows the men as they follow a stream through the Vietnamese jungle, highlighting their fear and tension as they hear strange noises and wonder if the enemy is following them. But the film also shows the mundane aspects of the platoon's daily life in Vietnam: one member of the platoon gets several days off and travels to Saigon, from which he returns to the platoon several days early because he has spent all of his money.

One of the first orders that Anderson received was to find an American helicopter in a region called the Central Highlands that had crashed during a mail drop. Anderson explained during an interview how nervous he was leading his men on this mission: "This was my first operation. I'm new in-country. People didn't know me. I don't know them. They have to be thinking, Can this platoon leader handle it? I was only a second lieutenant." Of course, Anderson also felt tension as being a young African American platoon leader of mostly white soldiers. He knew that he would be judged far more harshly than a white platoon leader, solely due to his race.

For this mission, Anderson led his men in a forced march across the Vietnamese countryside. After the sun set, Anderson led his men into a clear area, where they made sure the perimeter was clear and there were no enemies around. Then, they set up camp for the night. Anderson deliberately disobeyed orders in doing this. According to him, "Headquarters wanted me to keep moving and keep searching through the night. I knew it wasn't the smartest thing to do, because you could get ambushed. You can't see what you're doing in the dark." One of Anderson's strengths as a platoon leader was his ability to use his own intuition and reasoning to determine what was best for his men, even if this meant going against official orders. This would eventually make him a well-respected leader and friend to those men in his platoon.

Sure enough, there were enemies all around them. Anderson describes what happened next:

> *Around ten or eleven o'clock, they opened up on us. They were still there. We fought all night long until six in the morning. I learned very quickly how to call in artillery, how to put aircraft over me to drop flares and keep the area lighted up so they couldn't sneak up on me. I was calling the artillery in within 35, 40 yards of my own people, as tight as I could go without hitting us. I don't remember wondering if I was ever gonna get out of this. I just did not have time to think about it. I was just too busy directing fire to be scared.*

Anderson's platoon had been outnumbered ten to one by Viet Cong fighters during this battle. The Viet Cong eventually retreated under his fire. His soldiers then spread out and saved some injured American soldiers from a separate platoon. For both winning this battle and for rescuing his fellow soldiers, Anderson would receive a Silver Star, the US military's third-highest award for bravery in battle. But, even more important than this award, Anderson said, was the bond that it created between him and his men. He said, "It was my first chance to react under fire and it had gone well. My men knew I could handle the responsibility."

Unfortunately, not all of Anderson's men survived this battle. Bill Shannon, an eighteen-year-old soldier from California, lost his life, and another soldier was seriously injured. This battle, shown in *The Anderson Company*, served as the climax of the film. In this final scene, after the platoon comes under

these are people that you work with and get to know during extremely critical situations. There is no room for pretense. There is really no place or chance to practice racial discrimination because you're so closely knit.

AFTER VIETNAM

At the end of his service, Anderson was awarded two Silver Stars, five Bronze Stars, three Army Commendation Medals, and eleven Air Medals. In addition to earning an Oscar for best feature-length Documentary in 1967, *The Anderson Platoon* was also awarded an Emmy for best documentary film. After thirteen years of service and a promotion to Lieutenant Colonel, Anderson retired from the military. He

The Silver Star, awarded to Anderson, is one of the highest awards offered by the US military for valor in combat.

Lieutenant Colonel Anderson has gone on to have a successful business career in the years since the Vietnam War.

went on to earn two master's degrees from the University of California, Los Angeles.

After leaving Vietnam, Anderson went to work for a company where he managed military supplies and logistics for four platoons, or 130 men. Although he was no longer in

The Anderson Platoon

When *The Anderson Platoon* first came out in 1967, it drew a lot of attention for its depictions of a platoon led by a young black lieutenant. This is the beginning of an article in *Ebony* magazine, published in October 1967, which profiles Anderson and analyzes what would go on to become an important documentary about American soldiers fighting in the Vietnam War:

> *The Patrol was soaked from a pouring rain as it slowly made its way up to a deep stream while dodging bullets. Although the men were far from home in Viet Nam, the familiar soulful sound of the blues throbbed in the background echoing the mood: "It's so hard to keep from crying, but my heart feels just like lead …." Some were wounded. The man in charge, 24-year-old 1st Lt. Joseph B Anderson Jr. of Topeka, Kan., was a black man—he made the decisions for his weary men, both black and white.*

active duty, he used the skills he had learned over in Vietnam to launch a successful career. In 1977, Anderson spent time as a White House Fellow and worked with the Special Assistant to Secretary of Commerce. He spent two years working in policy before joining General Motors in manufacturing in 1979. Over the next ten years, Anderson would work his way to General Director of a business unit at General Motors, with seven thousand employees under him. In 1992, Anderson left General Motors to become President and Chief Executive Officer of Composite Energy Management Systems.

Anderson currently serves on the boards of several major corporations and was a member of the US Department of Commerce Manufacturing Council from 2013 until 2015. In 2007, Anderson received an Honorary Doctor of Management degree from Kettering University. In 2013, he received an Honorary Doctor of Commercial Science Degree from Central Michigan University.

Anderson had many different experiences throughout his life—from his experiences in Vietnam to his successful academic and business career afterward. But he credits all of his success to his work ethic and his "stick-to-itiveness." Anderson continues to work for increased diversity in the military through the For Us All Campaign, which works to make sure that African American cadets have the equal opportunities in the army that Anderson might have missed out on himself back when he was a cadet.

U.S.
McDANIEL

FOUR

Colonel Norman Alexander McDaniel

Like Lieutenant Joseph B. Anderson, Norman Alexander McDaniel is just one example of an African American who served with distinction in the Vietnam War. McDaniel's story is one of courage and perseverance in the face of dire circumstances.

Norman was born in Fayetteville, North Carolina, in 1937. His parents were Clyde Oliver McDaniel and Fannie Marie McDaniel. Norman was one of nine children and his family had been sharecroppers with little financial means. As such, McDaniel knew that his parents wouldn't be able to help pay for his education. He had plans from a young age, therefore, to join the military in order to get an education.

***Opposite*: Former prisoner of war Norman Alexander McDaniel smiles after arriving back in the United States in 1973.**

McDaniel completed training on a B-52 Stratofortress bomber, like the one shown here.

McDaniel graduated as the valedictorian of his class at Armstrong High School. He was well-liked and respected by both students and teachers alike. In fact, his teachers were so impressed with McDaniel that they helped him get a job at North Carolina Agricultural and Technical State University so that he could work his way through college in order to afford tuition. After four years, McDaniel graduated cum laude from college in 1959. As a member of the ROTC while at North Carolina Agricultural and Technical State University, he was a distinguished graduate. He then went on to serve in the United States Air Force as a second lieutenant. He was sent to the James Connally Air Force Base in Waco, Texas. He also went to Electronic Warfare Officer Training (EWO) at Keesler Air Force Base in Biloxi, Mississippi, and completed B-52 Stratofortress (a kind of strategic bomber) combat crew training.

CAPTURED

In 1966, McDaniel was sent to Southeast Asia, where he began flying combat missions from Takhli Royal Air Force Base in Thailand. He flew a Douglas EB66C Skywarrior, which was an electronic **reconnaissance** aircraft, along with four other crewmembers. However, during his forty-first mission on July 20, his plane was hit by enemy fire and he had to eject from the plane. He landed in North Vietnam, about 30 miles (48 km) north of Hanoi. As soon as his parachute landed on the ground, he was captured by the North Vietnamese as a **prisoner of war (POW)**.

He was taken along with other crewmembers from the flight, including Lawrence Barbay, William H. Maens, Edwin L. Hubbard, Glendon W. Perkins, and Craig R. Norbert. McDaniel was thirty-five years old when he was captured. He would stay a prisoner of war with the North Vietnamese for seven years, until 1973. Despite this, McDaniel would call himself "one of the luckiest of the unlucky." This was partly because, as McDaniel said, he almost went down with the plane. "If it had been a direct hit, I wouldn't be speaking with you now," McDaniel told an interviewer in 1999. "The missile detonated close to the airplane and some of the fragments punctured the fuel tanks."

When McDaniel was surrounded and captured, he had burns all over the left side of his body, a wound in his neck, and a sprained ankle. But the North Vietnamese did not take pity on him. In fact, as soon as he was transferred to a prison, he was tortured by his North Vietnamese captors. "They'd drag you out, beat you, slap you, kick you, then throw you back onto

McDaniel was kept at the largest North Vietnamese prison for POWs, sarcastically known as the "Hanoi Hilton."

the concrete slab in the dark cell," he recounted years later. "You'd lie there, not knowing if it's day or night, and doze off. You might think you were sleeping for two or three hours when you only slept for twenty minutes. Then they'd drag you back for another round of torture and interrogation."

At some point during his years in captivity, McDaniel did not believe that he would be able to survive any longer. The constant torture was almost too much to bear. Sometimes, McDaniel said, he asked to die because living was just "not worth it." The only thing that helped him survive these very difficult moments was thinking back on other American prisoners of war who had also experienced such dismal circumstances and came out on the other side. He said, "If some of them survived, I can, too. I've got to get back to my family."

What the North Vietnamese wanted was any military secrets or biographical information that McDaniel had. They tried everything to extract information from McDaniel, including, as he said, playing "the race card." He said:

> *They'd say, you're a black man, we're colored people and the United States is waging a war of genocide against colored people. They knew enough about the Black Panthers, officers being fragged by enlisted people in South Vietnam and the friction between black and white GIs in Europe to throw them in my face saying, "You must agree with us, help us." They wanted me to make propaganda appearances.*

But this did not affect McDaniel. Even when they called him an "Uncle Tom, lackey, and all that." He said, "I wasn't about to betray my oath or be disloyal to my country."

McDaniel described one particular instance during the winter of 1967 when he was tempted to give up information in order to stop the torture:

> *I was taken from my cell to an interrogation room. This interrogation was different from most of the previous ones. Usually it consisted of questions, threats, and torture, but never before the NVN POW Camp Commander. On this day, sitting beside the Camp Commander were his Chief Propaganda Officer and another lesser ranking military officer. The initial part of the interrogation was extremely friendly with the Camp Commander asking (through an interpreter) about my health and treatment. He proceeded to explain that the war was very tough for everyone with many people on both sides dying and being killed, it could last for many years and become*

McDaniel hugs his family tightly upon returning home after seven years of captivity in North Vietnam.

speakers and workshops for a wide range of audiences. McDaniel was motivated to begin this business to show others that they can accomplish anything in life, including living as a POW for seven years in the harshest of circumstances, as he did. He said, "[If] a person's values, priorities, commitment, and faith are right and strong, that person could endure as I did." Following surviving seven years in captivity, McDaniel knew that anything was possible with determination and courage.

In 1975, McDaniel wrote a memoir about his experience in the military and in captivity, titled *Yet Another Voice.* In it, McDaniel described his hardship as well as the welcoming he received when he came home. At this point in the war, returning POWs were lauded for their bravery. However, other African American POWs had different experiences. As scholar Tara T. Green writes, McDaniel's memoir reads differently than other memoirs written by African Americans in Vietnam. She says, "[His] stance resembles that of Booker T. Washington, who admonished African Americans to regard their trials (slavery, in particular) as a cauldron where their mettle had been formed." She later writes, "It is as if he desires to efface totally any sense of racial difference."

It is important to note that not everyone has similar experiences if they share the same racial background. McDaniel certainly experienced different challenges while in captivity as an African American airman. In fact, McDaniel was only one of several African American POWs held by the North Vietnamese at that time. According to former secretary of defense William S. Cohen, "The North Vietnamese tried to exploit examples of racism in our country to drive a wedge between Norman McDaniel and America. He refused. His

POW and Poet

Following his release, Norman McDaniel wrote many poems about his experiences as a prisoner of war over seven years in the notorious North Vietnamese prison, which was sarcastically called the "Hanoi Hilton." McDaniel has also written other poems about his experience in Vietnam, including poems "God is My Pilot" and "Anniversary Poem." The following poem is titled "My Plight":

As time goes by, I find no need to cry,
though fate has frowned upon my upturned face,
and happiness has mostly passed me by,
I still await the hand of saving grace.

For six long years I've sat behind these bars,
sometimes too cold, more often, too hot.
Through windows small at night, I watch the stars
And wonder why to me befell this lot.

To cry would seem to say that I am weak
though six long years detained, my strength
has wrest;
While oft' from here my fate looks naught but bleak,
Still, I must stand and try to meet the test.

I'm still a man, and though I'm badly bent,
I'll hope and strive until my life is spent.

captors had misjudged the courage of this man and the strength of the nation that produced him." It was perhaps McDaniel's experience as a black POW that made him more reticent to speak about racial tensions. Instead, McDaniel wanted to focus on how he and other POWs had survived nearly impossible circumstances to lead successful lives—no matter their race or ethnic background. As McDaniel stated during a ceremony held in his honor, "Those of us who have gone in harm's way, engaged in combat, and have been held as prisoners of war truly appreciate the importance and the value of life, the preciousness of freedom, and how fortunate we are to be citizens of the United States of America."

LATER CAREER

In 1987, McDaniel retired from the Air Force as a colonel. Immediately following his retirement, he began to work in the defense industry. Then, in 1991, he began a new career as professor of acquisition management and chair of the department at the Defense Acquisition University. He stayed there until 2006. For his service, McDaniel was awarded many honors, including a Silver Star Medal, a Purple Heart, a Distinguished Flying Cross, a Defense Superior Service Medal, and a Legion of Merit. McDaniel also works part-time as a facilitator of the Transition Assistance Program (TAP), which aids returning veterans adjust from military to civilian life. In fact, McDaniel benefited from a similar program to this after his return home in 1973. An air force escort had stayed with McDaniel during his first three weeks at home in order to provide support and answer any questions McDaniel might have. McDaniel credited this support—as well as his

Upon his return to the United States, McDaniel was awarded many honors and embarked on a new career as a professor at the Defense Acquisition University.

family—with his ability to successfully readjust to life at home, although it did take nearly one year for him to be comfortable at home again.

McDaniel continues to speak about how lucky Americans are to live in relative freedom and stability. He said, "As Americans we have a great deal for which to be thankful. In spite of the imperfections and shortcomings we are very fortunate to be Americans. Instead of nonconstructive criticism, we should do our part to further improve our country in all fields in order that our nation's worthwhile potential become realities." McDaniel has spoken out on many occasions following his release about the democratic values of the United States and the need to preserve these values. He has also spoken about the role religion played in his survival while in North Vietnam, joking, "You know the old saying, 'There aren't many atheists in foxholes.'"

Today, McDaniel lives with his wife in Maryland. They have two children and four grandchildren.

VIET
VETERANS
AGAINST
THE WAR
OUT

FIVE

A Hero's Welcome?

Vietnam was a notoriously difficult war for returning veterans. Throughout the course of the war, public opinion had changed so much that returning veterans—even if they had been drafted—were greeted with hostility and even viewed as traitors. As veteran Ken Moffett writes,

> *[When] soldiers returned home from World War II and the Korean War, they were treated as heroes. A euphoric atmosphere overtook the nation, and celebrations were held in their honor all around the country … Unfortunately, this was not the case when soldiers returned home from Vietnam. As a result of America's loss in Vietnam, there was a misperception that the men who fought there did not measure up to their predecessors in World War II and Korea.*

***Opposite*: Vietnam veterans march against the war in 1971. Many Vietnam vets returned home to little support from both the US government and their fellow Americans.**

Further complicating the situation was the fact that the Vietnam War had been covered extensively in the media. For the first time in America's history, families could gather around the television screen at home and watch footage from the war "over there." There were many television reports and documentaries about what soldiers faced abroad. Some of them, including the investigative work of Seymour Hersh, who first broke the massacre at My Lai, showed the negative sides of the war, which included war crimes, prostitution rings, and drug use. Thus, Moffett writes, "Unlike the hero status given to the returning soldiers from World War II, the soldiers that served in Vietnam were portrayed as baby killers, psychos, drug addicts, and war mongers." Even those who had been drafted into the war and had no choice about whether or not they would fight were viewed as traitors when they returned home to the United States.

Sometimes, veterans would just be arriving home to the United States when they would be attacked by people carrying banners and shouting anti-war slogans after they stepped off their flight home. There were even some publicized cases of veterans who were refused service in restaurants and other businesses. All of this only compounded the despair and the isolation that returning Vietnam veterans felt.

MINORITY VETERANS RETURN HOME

Returning minority soldiers had an especially difficult time back in the United States. For one thing, it was difficult returning home to continued inequality, especially after serving their country and putting their lives on the line. Clinical psychologist Dr. Napoleon N. Vaughn outlined the many challenges that

Returning African American veterans of the Vietnam War had a particularly difficult time readjusting to life back in the United States, where they still faced discrimination due to their race.

minority veterans faced in particular: "They feel alienated because they have put their lives on the line only to return home and find social conditions the same as when they left; there is no market for the skills they have learned in the military; many did not even receive rudimentary skills training. Because they were considered underachievers, they were put in combat units."

Vaughn continued, "The military becomes the average ghetto youth's 'college.' They enlisted because they could not find a job or because they were getting into trouble. These problems did not disappear and, potentially, only escalated when they returned back home to civilian life." The problems that led many minority soldiers to enlist in the first place—or that had made them more susceptible to the draft—had not been resolved when they returned back home. In fact, these issues became even more problematic when they returned home suffering trauma from the war and being unable to find jobs or experiencing the same amount of racial injustice and racism that they had faced before leaving for the war.

POST-TRAUMATIC STRESS DISORDER

Many veterans returned with **post-traumatic stress disorder**, or PTSD. PTSD is classified as a mental disorder and occurs after someone has experienced trauma, and particularly when one's life was in danger. For people with PTSD, daily life can bring with it "triggers" back to the past traumatic moment. For these people, they relive these traumas at any time, experiencing flashbacks and dreams that increase their anxiety and fear on a daily basis. For veterans with PTSD, their past trauma is not yet in the past and they continue to fear for their lives even once they are removed from a warzone and back at home.

PTSD was only classified as a mental disorder in the aftermath of Vietnam, when so many men returned from the warfront. This was because so many returning soldiers exhibited the same symptoms. According to one Vietnam veteran, Roy R.,

> *You can't take a nineteen-year-old brain and subject it to the constant threat of death or injury by rocket fire and expect it not to be affected … [One of the reasons for these high levels of PTSD was] there weren't any frontlines in Vietnam. If you were there, you were in it. Everyone had the opportunity to get killed. Rockets were regularly coming down on our heads, and we were constantly under fire.*

After spending one year in Vietnam, this soldier spent the next thirty years trying to grapple with his PTSD.

Diane Evans, who served as a US Army nurse in the war, continues to struggle with the effects of her one-year deployment in hospitals in Vung Tau and Pleiku. Her "war terrors … came back to her in dreams: bloodied faces and dismembered bodies of soldiers and children covered in third-degree burns, patients she treated and some she watched die." For some returning veterans, they experienced these symptoms right upon returning home, while others only experienced PTSD years later.

According to the Department of Veteran Affairs, women were twice as likely to experience PTSD during Vietnam

Female nurses who served in Vietnam were twice as likely as men to experience PTSD in the years following the war.

than men. Women also had a higher risk of experiencing sexual assault during their time in the military, which could also provoke PTSD. In general, minority veterans of the Vietnam War were much more likely to experience PTSD than their white counterparts. According to researchers, this could have been due "to psychological conflicts related to identification with the Vietnamese" as well as racial tensions before, during, and after their deployment. According to a 1990 study, 14 percent of white veterans returned home from Vietnam with PTSD, while 21 percent of African Americans and 28 percent of Hispanics did. Between 22 and 25 percent of American Indian Vietnam veterans experienced PTSD.

One of the reasons for this, according to clinical studies, is what psychologists call "race-related stressors." This meant that minority veterans didn't just experience typical military trauma, but also experienced trauma due to treatment received due to their race. For example, some minority soldiers were more likely to be shot at by their fellow Americans because they were mistaken for looking like the enemy. Others were harassed due to their race and if they expressed any sympathy with the Vietnamese either due to their background or their own racial struggles.

WOMEN VIETNAM VETERANS

Years later, many Vietnam veterans still not only experience PTSD but feel as if they have been forgotten, or as if their service has still not been recognized. While between five and seven thousand women served in Vietnam, for example, mostly as nurses, they feel that their service has been forgotten and was never appreciated in the first place. Women returning home from Vietnam were told to just "toughen up" and forget the trauma they had experienced, even if this had been sexual trauma during the war.

According to clinical psychologist Jeffrey Mann, "For women, there is very much a desire to conform to that

Many female nurses saw combat in the Vietnam War, although their contributions were largely ignored.

military culture … you are already a minority and there can be a tremendous pressure to conform, just to push it down and pretend it's not there."

Women were more likely, therefore, to experience different symptoms then men upon returning home from the war. While women were more likely to be overtly anxious and specifically avoid situations that reminded them of their traumatic wartime experience, men were more likely to cope with their emotions through the use of drugs and alcohol.

Women also had the additional burden of not being taken as seriously as men. Because 80 percent of the women serving in Vietnam were nurses, it was just assumed by many people that they didn't experience combat. However, that wasn't the case. Many nurses not only worked in hospitals but worked out on battlefields, rescuing patients even as bullets whizzed by their heads.

"We didn't have a gun, but we would crawl on the floor when bombs were going off to be sure our patients were taken care of," said Joan Furey, who worked as a nurse in Vietnam. "You never picked up a weapon, but you certainly understood what it was like to think about dying."

RACISM AND POLITICAL TURMOIL AT HOME

Psychologist Napoleon Vaughn conducted a study of African American veterans who returned home to Philadelphia following the war. He reached the following conclusions: "All had a negative attitude about the war in Vietnam and felt the black man should not be fighting it; … A strong sense of racial pride was expressed by all and they talked about wanting to better conditions in their neighborhood; … All expressed disenchantment with conditions they found at home on their return."

Some of the veterans he studied expressed their discontent with both the war and their treatment at home strongly. "I would never advise anyone to go into the Army," said Howard W. Barbour, who returned from one tour in Vietnam at the age of twenty-two with two Purple Hearts. "This is not a black man's war. I felt I was fighting two enemies, the Vietcong and the white man who was supposed to be on my side."

Twenty-one-year-old Elijah Lamon expressed similar feelings. "When I was in 'Nam," he said, "It was like fighting two wars, one with the man who was supposed to be your

veterans who had served in that war for their country did not receive these benefits—or did not receive the same benefits that were given to whites—largely due to discrimination from financial institutions who refused to loan to African Americans. However, more black veterans were offered and received GI benefits than black veterans returning from previous wars. Thus, while there were a great many changes for minorities—and particularly minority veterans—in the United States, the effects of previous policies of discrimination continued.

Also as opposed to previous wars, returning service members were, on average, younger than in all previous wars. The average age of US soldiers in Vietnam was only nineteen, while most soldiers during World War II and Korea were twenty-two. Additionally, for the first time during Vietnam, service members were not attached to particular units during their tours of duty. Rather, soldiers would have an individual tour of duty and move around much more or finish their tours at different times than those who had been in their unit. This meant that soldiers often felt more isolated in and after Vietnam than during previous wars. Oftentimes, they would return home alone without the support system of their platoon.

VIETNAM WAR MEMORIALS AND WORKS OF ART

But this doesn't mean that life after Vietnam was all negative. Many returning veterans went on to enjoy full and happy lives. They had families and continued to have close relationships with those they had fought with in the war. Many of them went on to be successful doctors, entrepreneurs, businessmen and women, artists, lawyers, and politicians. It took the American public a long time to grapple with the consequences of Vietnam and to "welcome home" their veterans.

Beginning in the 1980s, nearly ten years after the war, many Vietnam War memorials were financed and built in order to properly honor those who had fought and, in many cases, sacrificed their lives. Most notably, the Vietnam Veterans Memorial in Washington, DC, was built in 1982. It was built in order to honor US service members who died in Vietnam,

The Vietnam Veterans Memorial in Washington, DC

as well as those who remained missing in action after the war. The wall is made up of two nearly 247-foot (75 meter) long walls made of gabbro rock, placed at an angle to one another. They prominently feature the etched names of all those lost during the war. As of 2015, 58,307 names are etched into the memorial, including the names of eight women who lost their lives fighting for their country. It remains one of the most well-known memorials and a popular tourist destination for those who visit Washington, DC.

Works of art also attempted to grapple with the question of what happened after soldiers returned from Vietnam. Movies such as *Platoon*, released in 1986, focused on the experiences of soldiers in Vietnam and was based on the director's, Oliver Stone, actual experiences while serving in Vietnam. *Born on the Fourth of July*, also written and directed by Stone, was released in 1989 and became a box office hit with Tom Cruise starring in the lead role. Based on the autobiography of veteran Ron Kovic, it focused not only on his experienced in the war but returning home in 1969 and facing both the symptoms of post-traumatic stress disorder and the severe injury he received while in service in Vietnam.

These movies, like many other big blockbuster movies, did not highlight the experiences of minorities in the war, and focused on white men. Film critics have also pointed out that many of these well-known Vietnam War films uncritically showed racism and did not attempt to portray the varied experiences of minority soldiers in any real way. Wallace Terry, a black journalist who covered the Vietnam War, said that, "*Platoon* shows black as lazy, implying that they have to be pushed to fight or that they lack leadership ability." Some films, such as *Dead Presidents*, directed by Albert Hughes in 1995, delved into the experience of an African American man in Vietnam and adjusting back to civilian life after the war. However, the film portrays a stark spiral into drug use and crime after returning home to a country and a government that does not provide proper support to Vietnam veterans, and particularly to minority veterans.

Terry states that black men were often depicted as cowardly or lazy, and rarely as leaders in many mainstream films about Vietnam. He continued:

> *I'm not suggesting that blacks weren't cowardly. Some were, as were some whites. But we had our commanders and heroes too. Brigadier General Frederic Davison commanded the 199th Light Infantry Brigade, and in the same 25th Infantry Division in which Oliver Stone sets* Platoon *we had a battalion commander by the name of James "Ambush" Bradley. Then there was Captain Riley L. Pitts, the country's first black officer to receive the Congressional Medal of Honor. He died saving his men, both black and white. Altogether, twenty blacks won the Medal of Honor in Vietnam.*

Terry also describes how, despite the belief that many integrated units were "colorblind" during the war, this was not true. Oftentimes, black soldiers received medals and other commendations later than whites did, or did not receive the same awards as whites for equally brave service. According to Terry, in 1967, the black power movement developed in Vietnam and led to increased political action in Vietnam, a "war inside a war." This was when the military created so-called

Wallace Terry

Wallace Terry was born in 1938 in New York City. After growing up in Indianapolis, Indiana, he began to work as a journalist. In 1960, at the age of just nineteen, he was hired by the *Washington Post*. Several years later he got a job with *Time* magazine. Beginning in 1967, he was the bureau chief of *Time* in Saigon and the first black war correspondent permanently

Wallace Terry, shown here on the left, became the first African American war correspondent permanently stationed in Vietnam.

stationed in Vietnam. For several years, he covered many important battles, including battles of the Tet Offensive. During his first year in Vietnam, he wrote an article, "The Negro in Vietnam," to great critical success. After this, he set a goal to publish a book about black service members experiences in the war. Eventually, the book was published as *Bloods: An Oral History of the Vietnam War by Black Veterans* in 1984. It became a best seller and was nominated for a Pulitzer Prize. He also recorded tape of black soldiers on the battlefields of Vietnam and released it as *Guess Who's Coming Home: Black Fighting Men Recorded Live in Vietnam*. Terry passed away in 2003 at the age of sixty-five. His last book, *Missing Pages: Black Journalists of Modern America: An Oral History*, was published posthumously in 2007.

Brigadier General Frederic Davison (*center*), commanded the 199th Light Brigade during the Tet Offensive.

Watch and Action Committees, which were programs developed to increase race relations in the military that still exist today.

Despite these issues, however, Terry views the Vietnam War as a moment of tension that would change the course of minorities' lives in the military in subsequent years. He says:

> *I'm convinced part of Martin Luther King's dream came true in Vietnam. In his famous 1963 speech at the Lincoln Memorial he said he had a dream that one day the sons of former slaves and sons of slave owners would sit at the same table. That dream came true in only one place, the front lines of Vietnam … I'm talking about thousands of Americans who found their common humanity on the front, where they shared the last drop of water, where they gave their lives for each other. Certainly putting on a uniform doesn't wipe away racism, but despite what I've described, the Armed Forces during the war and even today is the most successfully integrated institution in our society.*

There is no doubt that the United States and its military have a long way to go in terms of ensuring racial equality. However, perhaps Martin Luther King Jr.'s dream did come true, in some small way, in Vietnam. Women and men, no matter their race, fought along side one another in the heat of the battle, where differences became erased and only a fight for their humanity remained.

Glossary

black power A sub-movement of the civil rights movement in the 1960s and 1970s that supported equal rights and political power for African Americans through a variety of different ways.

boycott To withdraw financial or social contributions to a company or organization in protest.

cadets Young trainees or students in the military.

civilians Those who are not in the armed forces or members of a police force.

civil rights movement A political and social struggle during the 1950s and 1960s for equal rights for black Americans.

Cold War A period of heightened tension between the communist Soviet Union and the democratic United States that lasted from 1945 until 1990.

communism A political and economic theory first posited by Karl Marx in which all goods are publically owned and each person works according to his or her ability and needs.

company A group of soldiers; the smallest group of an infantry battalion commanded by a major or a captain.

disenfranchised To have deprived someone of their rights, particularly regarding voting rights.

draft Compulsory military service.

GI Bill An American law passed in 1945 that provided educational and financial benefits for veterans of wars.

guerilla warfare A type of war that is characterized by smaller surprise attacks rather than large, organized battles.

Gulf of Tonkin Resolution Passed by the US Congress on August 10, 1964, this resolution provided approval for larger American military intervention in Vietnam.

Jim Crow laws State and local laws that reinforced the segregation of disenfranchisement of African Americans.

platoon A subdivision of a company, usually commanded by a lieutenant.

post-traumatic stress disorder (PTSD) A medical disorder first classified as such after the Vietnam War that causes those who have experienced trauma to feel extreme anxiety, depression, and fear and to continue to relive the traumatic experience long after the original trauma.

prisoner of war (POW) Any person who is captured by the military or government of a side in the war.

propaganda Oftentimes misleading information that is distributed purposefully by a government to increase support in their government policies or military campaigns.

reconnaissance The military observation of a particular area to find out secret information.

"separate but equal" doctrine A legal doctrine in the United States that stipulated that segregation of white and black Americans did not violate the Fourteenth Amendment, which guarantees equal rights to all American citizens.

shelling Bombing.

"silent majority" A term used by former president Richard Nixon to show his belief that most Americans supported the Vietnam War, even if they did not express this belief publically.

Soviet Union A nation in Eastern Europe made up of communist republics; its capital was Moscow.

Tet Offensive One of the largest military campaigns of the Vietnam, launched in 1968 by the North Vietnamese against the South Vietnamese.

tour A period of duty for military service.

Tuskegee airmen African-American military pilots who fought in World War II.

Viet Cong A communist guerilla group that fought against the South Vietnamese and their US allies.

Viet Minh Formed in 1945, a nationalist movement that fought against French rule in Vietnam.

Vietnamization The US policy of withdrawing American troops and transferring military responsibility to the South Vietnamese.

Bibliography

African-American Involvement in the Vietnam War: Veteran's Issues."Returning Veteran Attitudes." Retrieved January 18, 2017. http://www.aavw.org/served/vetsissues_attitudes_abstract07.html.

Astor, Gerald. *The Right to Fight: A History of African Americans in the Military*. Collingdale, PA: Diane Publishing Co, 1996.

Badalucco, Traci. "Vietnam Veterans Still Have PTSD 40 Years After War." *US News*, December 15, 2015. http://www.usnews.com/news/articles/2015/12/05/vietnam-veterans-still-have-ptsd-40-years-after-war.

Encyclopedia of the New American Nation. "The Vietnam War and Its Impact—American Veterans." Retrieved January 18, 2017. http://www.americanforeignrelations.com/O-W/The-Vietnam-War-and-Its-Impact-American-veterans.html.

Gallagher, Brendan. "The Vietnam War and the Civil Rights Movement." AR Net, February 20, 2014. http://www.americansc.org.uk/Online/Vietnam_Civil_Rights.htm.

Johnson, Collie J. "SECDEF Hosts DSMC Professor as Keynote Speaker, National POW/MIA Recognition Day." *Defense Acquisition University,* September–October 1998. http://www.dau.mil/pubscats/pubscats/pm/articles98/mcdanso.pdf.

McDaniel, Norman. "Vietnam." *A Gathering of Eagles by Colonel Jimmie Dean Coy (Ret).* Retrieved January 18, 2017. http://www.agatheringofeagles.com/stories/prisoners-of-hope-a-gathering-of-eagles/colonel-norman-mcdaniel-u-s-air-force-ret.

Meckley, Eric. "POWs Recall Captivity, Release from Vietnam." *The Daily Collegian, Pennsylvania State University*, October 9, 1989. http://www.collegian.psu.edu/arts_and_entertainment/article_39629ce0-f366-5054-b538-d5bec14ddf96.html.

Moffett, Ken. "Coming Home: A Study in Contrast." *Delta Winds: A Magazine of Study Essays*, 2001. Retrieved January 18, 2017. https://www.deltacollege.edu/org/deltawinds/DWOnline01/cominghome.html.

POW Network. "McDaniel, Norman Alexander." Retrieved January 18, 2017. http://www.pownetwork.org/bios/m/m102.htm.

Veterans, Inc. "Success Story: Roy." Retrieved January 1, 2017. http://www.veteransinc.org/services/housing-programs/roy.

Wilhelm, Maria. "An Angry Vietnam War Correspondent Charges that Black Combat Soldiers are Platoon's M.I.A's." *People*, April 20, 1987. http://people.com/archive/an-angry-vietnam-war-correspondent-charges-that-black-combat-soldiers-are-platoons-m-i-a-s-vol-27-no-16.

Further Information

Websites

African American Involvement in the Vietnam War

http://www.aavw.org

Learn more about African Americans who served in the Vietnam War through speeches and recordings, government documents, and newspaper clippings from the Vietnam era.

PBS: Battlefield Vietnam

http://www.pbs.org/battlefieldvietnam/history

This PBS site offers historical information about the time leading up to the Vietnam War, as well as the war itself.

Vietnam War Statistics

http://history-world.org/vietnam_war_statistics.htm

Explore statistical information about casualties, minorities serving, and other data involving American involvement in the Vietnam War.

Vietnam War Timeline

http://www.english.illinois.edu/maps/vietnam/timeline.htm

The University of Illinois offers a concise and helpful timeline of all important dates during the Vietnam War.

Books

Caputo, Philip. *A Rumor of War*. New York: Ballantine Books, 1994.

Edelman, Bernard, ed. *Dear America: Letters Home from Vietnam*. New York: W. W. Norton, 2002.

Hayslip, Le Ly. *When Heaven and Earth Changed Places*. New York: Plume, 1993.

Sherwood, John Darrell. *Black Sailor, White Navy: Racial Unrest in the Fleet during the Vietnam War Era*. New York: NYU Press, 2007.

Terry, Wallace. *Bloods: Black Veterans of the Vietnam War: An Oral History*. New York: Ballantine Books, 1985.

Westheider, James E. *Fighting on Two Fronts: African Americans and the Vietnam War*. New York: NYU Press, 1999.

Videos

***The Anderson Platoon*, 1967**

This documentary, directed by Pierre Schoendoerffer, follows the lives of Joseph B. Anderson and his men as they try to complete an important mission in Vietnam.

***Dead Presidents*, 1995**

This thriller follows the life of Vietnam War vet Anthony Curtis, who struggles with supporting himself and his family after returning home injured from the war and, thus, turns to a life of crime.

Index

Page numbers in **boldface** are illustrations. Entries in **boldface** are glossary terms.

About the Author

Elizabeth Schmermund is a writer, teacher, and scholar who studies the 2003 Iraq War and women in war. She enjoys writing on a range of topics for middle- and high-school students. She lives in New York with her family and enjoys discovering new books, hiking in the woods around her house, and looking for seashells on the beach with her son.